Live Life on Purpose
Discover what you were born to do

By Rachael L. Thompson

Introduction

When you ask children what they want to be when they grow up, they are full of ideas. They express their dreams without reservation or fear. Something changes as those children grow into adults. Most adults are working in a field not because it is their dream but because it is where they ended up. School led to internships led to connections led to jobs led to similar jobs. Weeks involve counting down the days until the weekend, with weekends being spent getting all the things done that didn't get accomplished during the week; rinse and repeat. It is time to stop this nonsense. Let the rest of the world live like robots, but take back your power to Live Life On Purpose!

A recent Work and Education poll (Gallup 2014) found that American salaried workers average 47 hours of work a week, with many other countries exceeding this average. Given the typical salaried employee gets two weeks of vacation, this averages to 2,350 hours of work each year. If you start at 18 and work until 65, this is over 110 thousand hours or over 12.5 full years of your life spent at work. If you are content spending 12 years of your life at your current job, congratulations! If this makes you a little sick to your stomach, read on.

This book does not provide career or business advice. You can find that plenty of other places. It instead gives you tools to break out of norms and unlearn everything you were taught to begin your path to discovering your true life purpose. You will learn all of the ways you were unknowingly shaped, all the ways you continue to screw yourself over, and how to make psychological and habitual changes that will take you on a path traveled only by a few.

I based everything in this book on my own personal experience. I found myself very unhappy, bored, and wanting more out of life so I decided to make a change. With degrees in psychology and clinical counseling, I have been trained to understand human thinking and behavior patterns. I simply applied this knowledge to help me change my own mindset and behavior in order to figure out what the hell I should do with my life. I recently went through this journey, made a lot of mistakes, and learned a lot of helpful tools. I was the

Guinea pig in my own personal experiment. I will use examples from my own journey to help explain differentconcepts, but this is not an autobiography. I share only to give you insight from someone who has actually gone through this process.

Use this book as a guide, but keep in mind you will only find success if you are willing to explore your ingrained beliefs, work to change your mindset and behavior patterns, try new techniques that may seem uncomfortable at first, and embark on a journey into the unknown. It may seem a little scary at first, but not nearly as scary as spending over 12 years of your life in unfulfilling complacency and unhappiness.

"Life is about learning, unlearning, and relearning."

Table of Contents

What is Life Purpose?	7
Part I: Learning and Unlearning	9
Chapter 1: Tell-Tale Signs You are NOT Living Your Life Purpose	11
Chapter 2: You Have Been Molded NOT to Live Your Life Purpose	13
Chapter 3: Five Steps to Discover How You Have Been Shaped	17
Chapter 4: Final Step in the Unlearning Process	21
Chapter 5: My Personal Experience	23
Chapter 6: Part I Conclusion	27
Part II: Relearning	29
Chapter 7: Understand Underlying Beliefs with Two Journaling Techniques	31
Chapter 8: Talk to Your Subconscious and Belief System	37
Chapter 9: Affirm You Are Awesome	39
Chapter 10: Explore All Likes, Dislikes, Strengths and Weaknesses	41

Chapter 11: Explore Core Values	43
Chapter 12: Create Your Idea List	45
Chapter 13: Research, Research, Research!	47
Chapter 14: Plan and Strategize for Success	49
Chapter 15: Set One Goal Each Day	51
Chapter 16: Build the Confidence to Succeed	55
Chapter 17: Try and Try Again	57
Part III: Methods to Guide this Process	59
Chapter 18: Visualize and Manifest Your New Life	61
Chapter 19: Six Powerful Meditation - Techniques	67
Chapter 20: Affirmations for Money, Success and Happiness	75
Chapter 21: Write a Letter to Yourself	79
Chapter 22: Find the Right Support	81
Chapter 23: Shhh! Keep Your Dreams a Secret at First	83
Chapter 24: Quick Recap	85
Conclusion	77
About the Author	89
References	97

What is Life Purpose?

If you lost something inside of your house, would you go to your front yard to find it? Silly question, right? Now consider a time that you wanted a solution to a problem. Where did you search? Probably online or asked friends and family for advice. We always look for answers to our problems outside of ourselves, through the advice of others, books, motivational speakers, or Google. We think if we can just find that perfect job, perfect partner, or perfect house all of our problems will be solved. These are all fine tactics to find solutions, however, when something is missing on the inside, we will never find it by looking outward. The purpose of this book is to turn on the lights in your 'house' and make it easier to find what you are looking for. The work of searching, however, is up to you.

What exactly are you searching for?

To find the answer to the posed question you must first unlearn almost everything that you know. After you have done this, you need to relearn new ways of acting and thinking that will lead you to your own answer. This unlearning and relearning is facilitated by introspection and reflection. Once you have your mind right, you can then try on various potential "life purposes" for size until you find the one that fits.

Forget that! I'm just going to take one of those aptitude or career tests to figure this out.

Sure, that might give you some interesting career choices to consider, and maybe you will find your ideal fit. I encourage you to do that in fact, but in addition take the time to do the exercises in this book. This is your life, and as far as we are certain, we only get this chance, in this body, to live the life we want. Even if you believe in reincarnation (and this book certainly does not delve into that), why would you want to wait until your next life to be the person you are meant to be. Start now!

The main direction of this book is to lead you to your ideal line of work. For many this will be an entrepreneurial lifestyle, while others may want to find their perfect job. It is written more for those who want to start a business but certainly can be used as a guide to finding the right career path. In this book, you will see the terms "life purpose", "true calling", "ideal fit", and a few others that are all simply meant to describe what you can do on a daily basis to reach your ultimate happiness and fulfillment.

PART I: Learning & Unlearning

It has been said that life is about learning, unlearning and relearning. This first section will focus on what and how you have learned up until this point in your life and also how to begin unlearning that which is not useful to you when accomplishing your life purpose. This section will focus on the following:

1. Signs that you are not living your life purpose
2. Concepts on how you have been shaped to think and behave
3. Discover specifically how your mindset affects you today
4. How to change dysfunctional thinking patterns

Chapter 1: Tell-Tale Signs You are NOT Living Your Life Purpose

Think now about your current situation. I'm assuming that it's not exactly what you want, leading to your interest in searching for your life purpose. Listed below are the top three indicators that you are not in a job, career or field you are meant to be in. This is your first chance to reflect on your situation. Knowing what is not a right fit and why will facilitate your progression on the path to find your life purpose.

1. *You are going against the grain:* When you engage in an activity you love, you will feel as if you are going with the grain, it feels smooth and unforced. This is not to say you will never run into any problems or have to deal with unpleasant situations. Think, however, on a day-to-day basis when you are doing the actual work (not the minute tasks that can get annoying but the actual work) does it feel smooth, effortless at times? If your work causes you to feel as if you are constantly moving uphill, going against the grain, or makes you wonder how other people actually seem to enjoy this type of work, you are not living your life purpose. Overall negative feelings towards your line of work will make each day a challenge filled with stress, worry, and general unhappiness. Think now, what in particular makes you unhappy about your current situation? Get as specific as you can so you are able to avoid these sources of unhappiness in the future.

2. *Indifference or Boredom:* Have you ever asked someone how their job was going and they replied with "I don't hate it." Perhaps this is how you feel about your current position. It is a common misconception that it is

acceptable to settle for a job that is just 'okay' because it is better than being in a job you hate. Although, there is some truth to this, do you really want to look back at your life and say "Well, I didn't hate it." I am sure not. You most likely would want to look back at your accomplishments, positive experiences, and the joys life had to offer you. Nowlistthe parts of your career that cause boredom and also contemplate what in life you feel passionate or excited about and why.

3. *Something Doesn't Feel Right:* Even if you like your job, for the most part, there can still be aspects that just don't feel right. A common aspect that is not satisfying for many in their current positions is their income potential. If you have thepotential to make more money doing something else, why stay in a job that is not giving you the financial freedom you desire? Or perhaps it is the work-life balance. Careers are only one component of life, and if this takes away from other things you enjoy, it is not your life purpose. It is misleading to believe, however, there will never be sacrifices in life, but if you are sacrificing on a daily or weekly basis, it is not bringing you the happiness and fulfillment possible. Use this as an opportunity for reflection. Examine what exactly feels off and consider options that will provide you with this missing piece.

Chapter 2: You Have Been Molded NOT to Live Your Life Purpose

There are a lot of learning theories based in psychology used to describe the many ways that humans learn how to navigate through life. To understand how you have been molded not to live your life purpose, it is essential to know some basic concepts that explain this molding process. The key concept discussed in this book is called *conditioning*;this is because when trying to figure out your life purpose you need to first let go of all of your conditioning that has gotten you to this point in your life. Conditioning can be defined as "a simple form of learning that involves the formation, strengthening and weakening of a response to stimulus" (merriam-webster.com). We are conditioned from birth, through either reinforcement or punishment, to behave in certain ways. This is how we learn what is appropriate and not appropriate.

There are two ways that behavior can be reinforced, or strengthened. Positive reinforcement encourages behaviors with rewards. If you bring home a good grade and your parents reward you with compliments or a gift, this is positive reinforcement. You continue to bring home good grades to get the positive reinforcement and after time the act of getting good grades becomes conditioned. There is also negative reinforcement in which you engage in behavior to avoid something negative. For example, you bring home good grades to avoid getting nagged by your mother. By adding both positive and negative reinforcement to a particular behavior (getting good grades) it becomes even further ingrained.

Another part of conditioning involves punishments, both positive and negative. Perhaps you once back-talked and got sent to time out, this is a positive punishment (something is added as a form of punishment). Or if you back-talked and your parents took away your favorite toy, this is negative punishment (something is taken away as a form of punishment). Through the combination of reinforcement and punishment, children learn how to think and behave and once conditioned will continue these patterns without even realizing it, possibly for the rest of their lives.

Not all behaviors and thoughts are directly conditioned and many can be learned through observation or being taught to you by others. You may have been told that if you do not go to college you will only get a minimum wage job and you believed it. You may have observed your older brother get in trouble for sneaking out and you learned not to sneak out. You may have also learned ways of behaving from observing how your parents and peers behaved. Everything you observed, were taught and that was conditioned combines to form your mindset and thinking and behavior patterns.

Conditioning and learning can be necessary to turn us into functioning members of society, but it also has its downfalls. Take a moment to think of how you were conditioned in your life. Did you ever want to be an astronaut and multiple people told you this was a silly idea? This is essentially positive punishment because they insulted you for sharing this idea. Or perhaps people praised you when you told them you were going to college. This is positive reinforcement for going to college. After enough conditioning, these thoughts became ingrained. You 'knew' you would never become an astronaut and you 'knew' you would go to college. In your conditioned brain, there were no other options.

You were raised and taught by people who most likely wanted the best for you but were conditioned, by people and events in their own lives, to hold certain beliefs. Your peers most likely learned to have a similar mindset because they too were conditioned by their parents and teachers who were previously conditioned to think and act in certain ways. It becomes a cycle in which one generation passes along mindsets, values, expectations and behaviors to the next generation with very few people taking time to evaluate their own learning process and assess if it actually makes sense.

Every society has norms and every culture within these societies has norms. Every subculture also has its own norms. For example, living in the U.S. has a set of norms by which citizens are conditioned to follow. Furthermore, there are plenty of different cultures within the U.S., which are determined by background, geographic location, ethnicity, and socioeconomic status. Within these cultures there are subcultures, which include family and community dynamics. A child raised in an upper-class, suburban, neighborhood in California, whose parents were first-generation immigrants from China with the occupations of a doctor and a lawyer, would have a different life experience than an African-American child, who grew up in the inner-city, with parents who were a minister and a social worker and moved to the city to help the community, would have a different experiencethan a Caucasian child, who grew up in a single-mother household, in a small southern town where the majority of the citizens worked in one factory, and whose family had been in the area for generations. Without jumping to any drastic conclusions, the first child may have been conditioned to get good grades and pursue higher education, the second child may have been conditioned to try to help others and the community, and the third child may have been conditioned to work hard and stay close to home. It is not to say that any upbringing is better than another, it is meant to show how upbringing can and often does shape a person's career and lifestyle choices.

Think about how your upbringing, environment, and societal norms shaped your views. What were your expectations? Were you raised to think you need a further education in order to be successful? Were you raised to think that you have to work hard just to get by? Were you raised to think that your only option is to get a job and work your eight or 12 hours a day to get the paycheck to support a simple life? What are your thoughts regarding money? Were you raised by parents who said people who made a lot of money were somehow bad? Were you told that the only way to be considered successful is if you earn a lot of money? Was there an emphasis to get good grades starting in kindergarten? Was there an emphasis on math and science or arts or athletics? When uncovering how you were shaped and how you were conditioned, you must start very young. Conditioning starts with your subconscious and the shaping of your subconscious begins at birth, before you even have memories. Before you can discover your life purpose, you must first recognize all the ways that you've been shaped. In the next chapter, you will get a chance to delve into each one of these areas separately.

Chapter 3: Five Steps to Discover How You Have Been Shaped

Hopefully, you have already begun to ask yourself some introspective and exploratory questions. These next five steps will help guide you through the key areas in which you may have been conditioned and how the conditioning could have affected your thoughts, feelings, and actions.

Remember, not all conditioning is 'bad' or has a negative effect. Much of your conditioning has turned you into the person you are today so do not try to change what is not broken. Also, do not think you must change your core values. Instead think of what beliefs have caused you distress, anxiety or led to unfavorable life choices. Reflect on your past and how your thoughts, interpretation of situations and personal actions or reactionshave caused roadblocks to your success and happiness. This is a very personal journey, and no two people will have the same perspective during this process. This is also not about blame (of yourself or others), rather recognition and change. Be gentle and honest with yourself as you go through this process.

There are five areas listed below in which everyone has different thoughts and beliefsthat have been learned and conditioned through various life experiences. Read each one slowly and think of how you have been shaped. Reflect on the thoughts and feelings you have in regards to each area, what you were told growing up, what you observed throughout your life, what behaviors were reinforced or punished, and how this lead to your decisions thus far. There are some leading questions listed in each area, but these are simply examples. Only you know your situation, so brainstorm all the ways you have been molded and how this has led you to the point you are at now. It would be very helpful to grab a pen and paper to write down all of your answers. You will be able to come back to these answers later when you work on shifting your thinking patterns.

1. *Profession:* Think of what you have been taught you should do "when you grow up" and reflect on how this has led to both major and minor decisions. Also, think about your beliefs and feelings surrounding careers and your chosen profession. Perhaps you were raised in a family of doctors, and you grew up knowing you should be in the medical profession. When you realized it wasn't a fit what did you think? Were you disappointed? Label yourself a failure? Try to talk yourself into pursuing it anyway? How did you family react or how do you think they will react when you tell them? Is there fear, rejection or other negative associations with this?

2. *Education:* Think about your conditioning related to education. Was there an emphasis on doing well scholastically? Did you struggle in school and thus labeled a 'bad student'? Was there a push to further your education after high school or to join the workforce? Think about how your life was shaped by this conditioning. Did you go to college when you really wanted to pursue something else? Were you always reluctant to get afurther education because you're 'just not good at school'?

3. *Money:* Think of how you were conditioned in regards to money. Were you lead to believe that "money does not grow on trees"? That only other people are rich? That you are expected to make a certain amount of money to be considered worthy or valuable in society? Depending on upbringing and experiences, everyone has different conditioned beliefs surrounding money. Now reflect on how they shaped your decisions and how they continue to shape the view you have of yourself in relation to money. Did you choose a profession based solely on its income potential? Do you always find yourself in low-paying jobs? Do people who earn a lot of money make you uncomfortable?

4. *Family:* What do you believe your role is in the family? Were you taught that men should be the sole financial providers and women should be more focused on family than career goals? What was your role in your family growing up? Were you oldest, youngest, middle child? What were your key responsibilities? Do you feel family obligations currently that prevent you from following your purpose? For example, perhaps you want to open a business that would thrive in California but feel obligated to stay close to your family in Kentucky. Or maybe you feel guilty that you want to start your own business because you have two young children.

5. *Pivotal Moments*: Finally, think about key moments in your life or key conversations that shaped your beliefs about what you can do. Did you ever tell a teacher or your parents you wanted to do something when you grew up, and they dismissed it? Did you switch your major in college because you failed a big test in one of your core classes? Too often it only takes one big event to lead us down a different life path and reshape our views of our capabilities.

Chapter 4: Final Step in the Un-learning Process: Do Not Allow Yourself or Others to Stop You

After you have examined your conditioning, observe how you are currently being affected by it. Observe your own self-talk and also how others react in different conversations, due to their conditioning and societal norms. If you allow others' doubts, your own doubts, your previous conditioning or negative thinking patterns to affect you, this will get in the way of discovering and pursuing what you are truly meant to do. Get clear on your thinking patterns and your own conditioning and recognize them as such. They are learned behaviors and thoughts, not the truth.

You also must stop allowing other's reactions to affect you negatively. Recognize that others around you may not understand your decisions and mindset and all of their doubts only stem from their own unfortunate ignorance and conditioning. The word "ignorance" is not meant in a condescending nor a judgmental manner; everyone is ignorant in certain aspects of life. I'm ignorant, you're ignorant, everybody is. Possibly you were ignorant about what conditioning meant and how you have been shaped before reading this. Many are simply unaware of their own conditioning and why they hold particular beliefs. This is fine and normal. Do not try to change anyone rather become aware of this common trait so that you don't allow others to deter you in your endeavors and personal growth.

Chapter 5: My Personal Experience

I want to share a bit about my experience as an illustration of my own conditioning and where it lead me. When reading this, I encourage you to put together the pieces of your own journey that have lead you to the place you are in now.

My Background: I came from a divorced home, with two Caucasian baby-boomer parents, who came from working class families and received higher education and worked white collar jobs (mother was a nurse and father an attorney). It was basically required that I get a higher education. Good grades, college, and eventually getting a white-collar job were the expectations, and I never questioned it.

My Conditioning: I always focused on my grades as I associated good grades with success and acceptance from others. I received praise from my parents and teachers which encouraged (positively reinforced) me to succeed in school. When my grades dropped in middle school, I got grounded and had to have a meeting with my teachers, which was all terrible (positive punishment), so I brought them back up and kept them there. I, of course, went to college and earned both a Bachelors and a Masters degree. During higher education I primarily focused on getting good grades, thinking that when I graduated, I would easily get a good, decent-paying job (what I had been told by parents and society). I was also conditioned to think that if I put my mind to something and if I worked hard enough it would pay off.

Reality Check: After I had received my Masters, I found that although I enjoyed learning about my field, I did not enjoy actually working in it. I also realized the hard truth that it would never pay as much as I wanted. My bubble was officially burst after these realizations. Everything I had been conditioned to believe, was not my reality. I got a job that sucked the life out of me every day. In talking to others, I was not the minority, but people felt stuck in these jobs because they had financial responsibilities. Was this going to be my life forever?

Questioning Norms& Conditioning: I was not going to settle working solely for a paycheck. I began to wonder what I should be doing because I knew that being unhappy and bored every day was not the life I wanted. Another thing I was led to believe is that I would never make a lot of money, other people could be rich, but that was just not in the cards for me. My mother, who grew up fairly poor, reinforced this idea unintentionally while we were growing up. I also believed that owning my own business was not something I was capable of doing because I didn't know how to do it. Again, my only conditioning was to get a professional job, not become an entrepreneur. I had to learn to let go of these conditioned ideas in order to embark on my life purpose journey.

My Unlearning & Relearning Process: It took a lot of work on a subconscious level, involving meditation techniques, affirmations, and journaling, for me to begin to overcome beliefs that had been conditioned for 30 years. Once I broke out these thinking patterns I was able to see the world in a new light. I was able to also see how other people had exactly the same thinking patterns that I had. Another realization during my process is that not everything you put work towards will be a giant success. Since I was used to this during all of my schooling, it came as a shock whenever I started a business, and it wasn't an immediate success. However, in retrospect, I realize that this was not in line with what I was supposed to do, and I'm grateful as this taught me a lot of lessons.

Facing Pressure from Others: I had to face pressures from others who had been conditioned to think that if something does not work out as planned, it is a failure.I found it really hard to communicate what I was feeling in my gut and that I knew my first business attempt was not a failure but a lesson.I even began doubting myself and felt pressure to prove to others I was going to be successful. I had to stop my negative thinking and remind myself of my truth, and not allow societal pressures to influence my decisions. Every step, either being a success or failure or somewhere in between, has led me closer to my end goal of living my life purpose. I continue to learn, and every milestone was an opportunity for introspection. I cannot blame others for making me feel bad or pressuring me, as their view of the situation had been skewed due to their own ingrained conditioning. I now keep my successes and hurdles to myself and confide in a few people close to me, which has worked much better for my psyche and made me more successful as I stopped letting others influence my work.

I share my personal journey only as an example of a common pattern in which one is first conditioned, acts in a way that is congruent with this conditioning, breaks free of it when it causes unhappiness and dealswith societal pressures as one embarks on a journey that is not the norm. Now let's look at how you can begin your process.

Chapter 6: Unlearning Conclusion

I hope that you have begun to reflect on your current situation, how you got here and maybe even started to get ideas of where you might want to go in the future. It will take a lot of reflection through journaling, meditation or various other methods of introspection (discussed in the subsequent chapters) to understand your conditioned beliefs and mindset. Once you have an understanding, you can begin to change all the detrimental beliefs that are holding you back.

Ideally, you also now understand that unhealthy beliefs are based on what others have told you and experiences that you had, but they're not the truth. Once you have gained this understanding, you can begin to discover, in an unbiased manner, your true life purpose. Remember that it took years for you to be conditioned in a particular manner and changing these beliefs will not happen overnight. This process may seem daunting, but it is the first step to a better life.

This "Unlearning" section has provided theories and examples to encourage an understanding of the complexity of your situation. In the next section, you will learn techniques to help you change belief patterns and start exploring potential career and business ideas that align perfectly with your true calling.

PART II: Relearning

Process Overview

Hopefully, you now understand all that has led to this point in your life. The second part of the book will focus on moving you closer to your desired life by helping you:

1. Get to the root cause of unhealthy beliefs
2. Change these belief patterns
3. Replace unproductive belief patterns with healthy ones
4. Organize values, interests, and strengths
5. With new mindset, brainstorm possible business or career ideas
6. Research ideas to find the right fit
7. Strategize and plan for success
8. Build confidence and eliminate fear

Chapter 7: Understand Underlying Beliefs with Two Journaling Techniques

It can be insightful and cathartic to express and organize all of your thoughts onto paper. There are multiple ways that you can journal, but two specific techniques will be illustrated to facilitate the process of understanding and changing unhealthy thinking patterns.

<u>Technique One</u>

The first technique is the *Free-Writing Technique.* This is when you simply write down all of your thoughts on a particular topic. Do not worry if they make sense and do not censor yourself. We spend our lives censoring what we say around others as not to say anything offensive or potentially off-putting. This is your time to allow yourself a freedom that has been inhibited for a lifetime. After you are done, tear up the paper, burn it, do whatever you want and know that this is an exercise just between you and the paper.

Start with a topic and go. Write until you feel you cannot write anymore. After you have completed this process, take a break. Do something to distract your mind and ideally get your body moving (go for a walk, do the dishes, take a shower). Then come back to what you wrote and read it. You can even use a highlighter or underline parts that you want to remember or seem pivotal. You can do this with any topic or multiple topics.

Some examples of questions you can ask are: What is my life purpose? What do I want to do? What is my perfect job? Or more specific questions like: What are my core values? What do I like about my current job? What do I hate about my current job? If you feel better talking things through, record yourself and play it back or dictate your thoughts and read them back. (There are plenty of free Apps available for both dictation and recording.)

Let's look at two examples. The first will help you uncover major dysfunctional thinking patterns while the second can be used to help discover what your true calling may be.

Example One: Free-Writing to Understand Beliefs

Why have I not been successful?

I am dumb. Nobody in my family has been successful. I have bad ideas. I have not had encouragement. My friends do not understand why I want to be successful. I should be happy with the simple things. Why do I even want more in life? Do I really deserve more in life?

As you can see with this example, the person has freely written some major beliefs that have been conditioned. The next step would be to then get to the root cause of each of these beliefs and eventually change them. (The second journaling technique will help with this process.)

Example Two: Free-Writing to Brainstorm Ideas

What is my life purpose?

I don't know. It hate it. I hate others who are happy with their lives. Was I ever happy? Yeah, I was in elementary school. Only because I had no responsibilities and got to play sports. I miss baseball. I miss my childhood. If I could play baseball or watch baseball all day, I would be happy. I know more about baseball than anyone I know. Should have been a sports reporter. I could do it better than anyone. All the reporters are idiots these days. I wish I would have gotten a degree. If only I had that, Icould have been a journalist and been paid to watch sports and give my commentary.

As you can see, this was a free flowing paragraph without any structure and without being polite or censored. It got out some underlying beliefs as well as a possible insight into what this person could begin to pursue. The goal of this is not to solve all of your problems or get the major answer to happiness. Instead, it is meant to shine alight on beliefs and take you from a place of unknowing to a state in which you can begin generating ideas. Perhaps this person could begin to explore jobs or professionsthat involve baseball. Perhaps a blog.Maybe become a little league coach. Possibly he can strive to write for a local newspaper or begin writing books about baseball. Some options may be more feasible than others, and some may be possible career options while others are more hobbies. He could repeat this exercise to brainstorm all the things he could possibly do within the baseball field. He could also expand this brainstorming to think of elements of baseball, such as being physically active, being part of a team, etc. to understand what elements of careers would make him the happiest. No matter what he chooses to do next, he is one step closer to discovering his life purpose.

Technique Two

The second journaling technique can be used to gain a deeper understanding of core thoughts and beliefs. If you have done the first journaling technique and found some themes in your thinking, this will be a helpful next step. This technique will help you understand what can be interfering with your success on a conscious or subconscious level.Some of these conditioned thinking patterns may be easy to spot while others function on a more subconscious level and you will need to dive deep to get to the root cause. This is where the *Questioning Technique* comes into play. In this technique, you will question yourself again and again until you understand the core belief behind your thinking. Once you know this core belief, you can then begin to disprove it and change it. If you effectively change dysfunctional, subconscious beliefs, you can change behaviors and get the results you long for in life. Let's illustrate this with an example:

I will never make a lot of money.

Why?

Because I just won't.

Why?

Because nobody in my family has been able to.

Why?

Because they are working class people.

Why?

Because they weren't smart enough to go to college.

Why?

We are just not a smart family. We don't do well in school but are hard, working-class people.

CORE THOUGHT: *I am not smart enough to make a lot of money. I am a hard-worker, and that is all I am good at.*

Once you are aware of the core thought that has been ingrained in your subconscious you can begin to change it. Disprove this thought in as many ways as you can.

Using the above example, the person could list all the ways in which they are smart. *I am smart in many areas, such as X, Y, and Z.*

They could then disprove their belief that *you have to do well in school to be a success* by simply affirming: *Plenty of successful people did not graduate college. (Finds names and list them.)*

Next, think of thoughts to replace your previous negative thinking and dysfunctional belief. Do not worry if you do not believe the statement at first. In a later chapter, we will go more in depth about restructuring beliefs. For now, just pick a few statements that positively contradict the beliefs you want to change.

For the example, the person might state:*I am smart. I am capable. I am able to run a successful business. I am able to make a lot of money.*

Chapter 8: Talk to Your Subconscious and Belief System

After you discovered some of the core beliefs that are holding you back, you have to work to change these beliefs to prevent them from continuing to inhibit your true potential. A technique, discussed by Dr. Cathy Collautt, is to have a frank conversation with yourself, in particular your subconscious. It can be helpful to get into a meditative state, and calm your mind before doing this. You can journal this conversation or simply talk to your subconscious, either aloud or silently in your mind. Proceed as if you are talking to a loving caregiver, who only wants the best for you but is going about it in the wrong way. Your subconscious is essentially trying to protect you from hurt, rejection, pain, sadness, disappointment, and the uncertainty of change. Understand this and do not get mad or upset that you hold unwantedbeliefs. Understand that your beliefs have been conditioned and may have kept you safe in the past. Be gentle yet strong in this conversation. Express to your subconsciousthat you understand why you developed and hold these beliefs. Next, let your subconscious know that you no longer need to hold this belief and promise it that if you can let go of these beliefs, you can live a better, happier, more successful life. Give your subconscious reasons why you are going to change these thoughts and the beliefsand how your new beliefs will only be beneficial.

Example of a Written Conversation with your Subconscious:

Belief: *Taking risks will hurt me.*

Dear Self...

I understand that you were conditioned to believe that taking risks will hurt me because this was something told to you from a very young age. Mom told you this because she suffered from anxiety and did not want you to get hurt. It was further reinforced when Uncle Tim was in a fatal accident riding his motorcycle without a helmet. It was again reinforced when dad lost his business because he took a risk.

I appreciate that you have kept me safe all of these years and prevented me from taking risks that would put me in danger. As of now, I will not do anything that is going to put myself in danger and if we can let go of this belief my life will be a lot happier.

If I take a risk to start a business, I promise that I am strong enough to face anything that arises. I am prepared to take this risk because I am smart, I have a well-researched plan and idea, and know this will make me happy and fulfilled.

This process is not going to instantly and automatically cure you of all your unwanted, automatic thoughts and it may need to be done on a frequent basis, in addition to other techniques, to transform these ingrained beliefs. It essentially helps you express that you understand where your beliefsoriginated, what reinforced these beliefs, and all the benefits of letting them go. After this conversation, you will more easily be able to spot these dysfunctional beliefsrevealing themselves in your life, understand they are not based in reality but in your mind, and continue to change them.

Chapter 9: Affirm You Are Awesome

An affirmation is the declaration that something exists or is true. These are simple statements that help to change your conditioned beliefs. Many people swear by affirmations while some doubt their ability to make a difference. If you have conditioned beliefs that you are trying to change, changing them with another belief that is more truthful or a belief that you want to become truthful, will only benefit you in your journey. For example, if you believe you are a failure, anaffirmation that can replace this would be "I am a success" or "I am working towards success". Know that you will not always believe these statements at first. Try to add the feeling of the affirmation when saying it. Feel the bodily and emotional sensations of success each time you say "I am a success". Perhaps you feel a release of tension, a warmth of pride in your chest, and a happy smile widening across your face. Think now of affirmations that you can use to help change your beliefs. Once you develop a list, say these to yourself frequently and anytime a negative thought tries to creep into your consciousness.

Beware of the ego! The ego is our sense of self. Psychoanalysis explains this as mediator between our subconscious and conscious, between our ID (basic instincts) and our Superego (morals and values). Our ego helps us navigate through the world. All of your conditioning and experiences, good and bad, helped this form and it will do anything to preserve itself. Know that your ego resists change and will try to tell you that your new thoughts and affirmations are incorrect. Acknowledge this resistance as the ego and recognize there is no truth to it. Look at it as your lower self, as a small child who throws a tantrum because he is scared to try something different. If your five-year-old child threw a tantrum because he did not want to go to school, would you say "Fine, you really don't need an education anyway"? No. You would reassure the child that everything will be okay, this experience will be good for him and make him go. Treat your ego as you would this child.

Understand the confirmation bias. The confirmation bias is the tendency to interpret new evidence as confirming current beliefs. You will both notice and remember instances, situations, events, andconversations that confirm your current beliefs and will more easily dismiss those that do not. If you believe you are a failure, you will remember each time that you failed, pay far more attention to perceived failures and easily dismiss any successes. When trying to change old and develop new beliefs,you must become aware of this confirmation bias. It will not be easy to focus on success when you are used to focusing on failures, so you must be diligent to focus on any success, not matter how small, and stop labeling failures as such. Be mindful of how you automatically label experiences and change these labels when necessary. For example, if you did not get a job that you interviewed for, your immediate response will likely be negative self-talk that confirms you are a failure. Be mindful of this, and replace these thoughts with more positive ones. This one situation does not define you as a failure. Think of what you excelled at during the interview and continue to affirm that you are working towards success. You can still hold yourself accountable and work to develop particular interview techniques that need improvement, but do not allow the negative aspects of the situation to skew the perception you are trying to develop for yourself.

Use these techniques (affirmations, challenging the ego and refuting negatively biased views) to get rid of all the beliefs that are holding you back and replace these with ones that will lead your life in your desired direction. It is not until you are free of these limiting beliefs that you will be able to pursue your life purpose. Once you are free, you will be able to naturally think and act in ways that encourage a truly happy and successful life.

Chapter 10: Explore All Likes, Dislikes, Strengths and Weaknesses

Once you have done all of the subconscious work, you can finally begin to explore what career or business will lead to happiness and fulfillment. For this it helps to brainstorm general likes, dislikes, strengths and weaknesses. Use both the *Free-Writing* and *Questioning Journal Techniques* to facilitate in this process. After getting a general idea of your likes/dislikes/strengths/weaknesses, try to get even more specific. For example, if you like working with people, ask yourself specifically what about working with people you like. Perhaps you like making people happy, and even more specifically you like to help others increase their confidence and self-esteem. The deeper you can dive into this exercise, the more benefit you will experience.

You can break it down even further into different jobs you have held, your hobbies (both past and present), school subjects, social situations, etc. Think about what you specifically liked and disliked in each job you held, each hobby you engaged in, and all of your classes from elementary school through the highest education you received. Be mindful, however, of how your outside experiences shaped your perceptions. Be exceptionally careful of what you have been told were your strengths and weaknesses. Were you told that "girls aren't good at math" or "boys shouldn't like art"? If you were told something at a certain age it may havebecome a self-fulfilling prophecy. An example from my own life is my belief that "I don't like math." I actually did like math, and excelled in it. None of my friends in school liked math, I was told I was better at language arts, and that math-related jobs were always boring, so I never considered a career involving any type of mathematics. Upon reflection, I do like math, but not all aspects. The particular aspect I like isthat there are set formulas for everything and I enjoyed figuring out how to use the formula to get the answer. I could add to my likes "Problem solving following formulas". In this example, you can see that I recognized I had been shaped by society and then explored what about this particular subject I enjoyed. Try to use a similar process in all areas as you work through this exercise.

Use the following exercise as guidance to explore your likes/dislikes/strengths/weaknesses:

Jobs/Careers

Likes:

Dislikes:

Strengths:

Weakness:

School:

Likes:

Dislikes:

Strengths:

Weaknesses:

Hobbies:

Likes:

Dislikes:

Strengths:

Weaknesses:

Overall:

Likes:

Dislikes:

Strengths:

Weaknesses:

Chapter 11: Explore Core Values

Finding a business or career that aligns with your value system is as important to your happiness as finding one that aligns with your interests. Understanding what you value most in life will help guide you to make the best decisions for your life purpose. This is, again, a time to be extremely honest and reflective. Do not allow any societal norms about work-ethic, money, family and responsibilities, to affect this assessment. If you value free time more than money, that is fine. If you value money more than family, that is also fine. These are your values. There must, of course, be the considerationof who you may affect (children, spouse, or family)with the decisions made based on these values and you may have to compromise some but for the sake of this exercise ponder what your true core values are. If you are unsure what your main values are, ask yourself some of the following questions: When am I most happy? When am I most proud? What do I want more than anything else? What would my perfect day look like?

Some common values are: Family, freedom, purpose, success, recognition, honesty, money, respect, love, creativity, innovation, adventure, helping others, making an impact, fun

Write down your top 3-5 values now...

Chapter 12: Create Your Idea List

Using both the brainstorming you did about your interests and values, begin to brainstorm ideas for businesses or careers you could pursue. Put together an idea list of 5-10 options. This can be in one field or various fields. For example, if you are interested in fitness you can put a list together of businesses within this field (i.e., Personal trainer, fitness blogger, health coach, design workout clothes, yoga instructor). Or if you are multi-passionate your list may look like *Fiction Author, Jewelry Designer, Interior Designer, Dog Trainer, Make-Up Artist*. Make sure that everything on your list is based on your likes, dislikes, strengths, weaknesses, and value system. Be honest with yourself about how closely these ideas align with the above factors. If you realize that one of your ideas does not align with one or more of the factors, explore what components of that idea you like and ask yourself if you can find similar components with another business that is in closer alignment. For example, if one of your ideas is health coaching but you know this will be hard to do with the traveling and freedom you value, you can explore the aspects of health coaching that intrigue and interest you and brainstorm other fields that will allow for this freedom. Perhaps you are passionate about helping people live a healthier lifestyle, well you could write books, blogs, create videos, all of which you can do from anywhere without sacrificing your freedom.

Chapter 13: Research, Research, Research!

Now that you have aclear picture of your likes, dislikes, values and possible ideas of things you want to do, this is the time to research. The more you can learn about different businesses and career options, the better. Keep a completely open mind. Talk to people who are in the field you want to enter. Get a part-time job or volunteer in this field. Read blogs and books, find websites, explore YouTube, and sign-up to email lists of people already doing what you want to do.

Get information on the following:

Typical job duties or business responsibilities

Training or educational requirements. For jobs, this would be formal education and experience and for business pursuits, it is the knowledge/education you need to gain to successfully start and run the business.

Job or business outlook

Earning Potential

Time Commitment

General idea of what your days and weeks will look like.

Chapter 14: Plan and Strategize for Success

Once you have an idea of what you want to pursue, devise a plan for how you will do this. Start small. Write down you overall goal and then break this down into the necessary steps you need to take to reach this end goal.

If you are still undecided, try to gain more knowledge and experience in potential fields that interest you. For example, if you are interested in entering the Health and Fitness field, you can start a weekly nutrition blog, while personal training a couple of clients and health coaching a few clients online each week. Perhaps you can build a business on all three or find that one is the best fit and most successful. If you want to enter the pet industry, you could get a part-time job at a doggy daycare, one at a pet boutique, and do some dog walking on the side. This way to can learn the ins and outs of the businesses and decide what the best fit is for you. Just make sure not to develop "shiny object syndrome" in which you constantly move onto the next, new opportunity. The purpose of trying several different things is to understand what will make you happy, have the highest chance of success, and what best aligns with your values, interests, and strengths. Remember that businesses take a while to become successful so do not get discouraged if you do not find immediate success. If you try something that you love, keep with it and continue to research ways to increase your chances of success. Too many quit, right before they reach the success they yearned for.

If you know what you want to pursue, begin to plan your business or career strategy. Make the decision of where you want to be in a year and break this down into smaller steps. A typical way to break down yearly goals is to develop quarterly plans. At the end of each quarter, re-asses and make adjustments to your plan as needed. The purpose of a plan is to help keep you on track. It is very easy to say what you want to do, but without concrete planning, it will be even easier to allow life to get in the way and procrastinate working towards your goals.

Chapter 15: Set One Goal Each Day

Once you have a quarterly plan strategized, become diligent about setting daily goals for yourself to help encourage continuous progress. Plan at least 3 days in advance for one goal you want to accomplish each day. Having your goals planned out in advance will help you stay on track and make it less tempting to get sidetracked or to procrastinate, but be flexible with yourself and make adjustments to your plans when necessary.

Working towards your life purpose can seem daunting and finding a place to start prevents many from making any progress. Setting just one small, daily goal gets the ball rolling and helps you build and keep momentum during this journey. Writing goals down will not only help you remember but also help to hold you accountable. You can write each daily goal in a planner, put it in your phone, or on your Google or Outlook calendar.

Tips on Goal-Setting: Good vs. Bad Goals

When making goals, keep the acronym SMART in mind. This will guide you in setting specific and actionable goals. This SMART goal guide will help break down huge, overwhelming goals into small ones that you can easily accomplish. Try to break every goal down to make sure that it is as SMART as possible, using the following guide.

SMART GOALS:

S: Specific - The goal is as detailed and clear as possible.

M: Measurable - The goal can be measured numerically.

A: Attainable & Actionable - You will be able to achieve this goal and take action on it today.

R: Relevant & Realistic - The goal is relevant to your overall plan and will be realistic for you to accomplish.

T: Time-bound - The goal has a start and end time that it must be accomplished by.

Now let's look at a broad (bad) goal compared to a SMART goal.

An example of bad goal: Learn more about business.

An example of a SMART goal: Read 1 business book (Specific and Measurable) by the end of this week (Time-Bound). It is also something that you can take action on and is relevant to your over-arching goal. Only you will know if it is attainable and realistic for you.

The next step is to break down the SMART goal into actionable steps and plan how you will accomplish this goal. If you are going to buy a business book, then the first step may be to research books by looking on Amazon and reading book descriptions and reviews. The second step would be placing an order for the book you decide on. The third step would be to set time aside to read this book, perhaps for an hour each evening. Goals, no matter how great, will not mean anything unless you have a clear plan of how you will work towards accomplishing them.

Below are three questions you can answer to help figure out what the next goal will be in your journey.

1) What is your final goal? Or, if you are unsure, what is your goal for the next month?

2) What are the big steps to get to this goal?

3) What is one goal that you can set today?

Look at the following example to get some ideas of where to start:

What is your final goal? Or, if you are unsure, what is your goal for the next month?

To open a hair salon

What are the big steps to get to this goal?

1. *Learn business basics*
2. *Figure out financing*
3. *Develop business model*
4. *Find location*

What is one goal that you can set today?

Sign up for an online basic business course by theend of today.

This person was clear that she wanted to open a salon and set up some basic goals she thought would lead her to this. Throughout her journey, these goals will likely change and become more concrete and detailed, but this is an excellent starting point. In this process, she figured out that the goal she could accomplish today was to sign up for a business course. After she has found a good course, she can make additional SMART goals to help her complete the business course and apply what she has learned.

When making your daily goals, keep the SMART acronym in mind. Anytime a goal seems intimidating, use this technique to break it down and prevent it from becoming overwhelming.

Chapter 16: Build the Confidence to Succeed

Say Goodbye to "Buts" and "What ifs"

The most crucial step in achieving the life you desire is to take action. This can be frightening for many. You can always create a story in your head filled with "but..." and "what if..." and end up talking yourself out of taking any action. Those who remain in a state that lacks fulfillment do so not because they are incapable of achieving success but rather because it is safe, and safety is easier than taking risks. Think of a time that you created a story in your head and the reality was nothing like that story. How many times in your life did you talk yourself out of something that could have been amazing?

The psychological term cognitive distortion is used to describe this type of thinking. Cognitive distortions are inaccurate thoughts that support negative thinking and emotions that disguise themselves as rational thoughts. There are plenty of different distortions that will prevent you from taking action by causing irrational feelings of fear, anxiety, and worry. Two become prevalent when faced with making drastic life changes. The first is called *fortune telling,* in which the person predicts a negative outcome without realistically considering the odds. Have you ever been convinced of how something would end? Think now of how many times you were actually right about the ending, especially when stakes and stress were high. Probably, not often.If you ever predicted how something would end and in reality, it actually ended this way, you will remember this time more than times you wrongly predicted the outcome due to your cognitive bias (as discussed earlier). A second distortion to watch out for is *catastrophizing,* which occurs when you look to the future and predict all of the worst case scenarios or when your mind makes an irrational catastrophe out of the current situation. For example, your boss doesn't speak to you in the morning, and you immediately think that you must have done something terribly wrong and will get fired. In actuality, your boss had an argument with her husband that morning and was upset about it, and you worried for no reason. This is the same as thinking that you will fail at a business pursuit or will never discover your life purpose. You have no actual facts to back this up, but the thought seems logical and will affect your actions if you let it.

Be aware of these distortions and realize that they are negative thinking patterns, in disguise. The truth is you will never know how a situation will turn out until you try. Some "failures" are only taking you a step closer to success if you let them. Have you ever taken a risk, even a small one, and were grateful you did? Remind yourself of these times when any distorted thoughts creep into your mind.

Chapter 17: Try and Try Again

It is hard to understand what various businesses and jobs will be like until you actually experience working in the field. Gain as much experience as you can and remember that there are no failures just lessons. Perhaps through reflection and research you decide that a particular field is likely your life purpose, but once you try it, you realize that it brings you very little enjoyment, and there are many aspects that you dislike. Great! This means you are one step closer to knowing what you are truly meant to be doing. You will never know unless you take the leap and try. It took Thomas Edison thousands of attempts to invent the lightbulb and when asked about all of his 'failures' he responded with "I have not failed. I've just found 10,000 ways that won't work."

There were many aspects of my first business venture that I enjoyed but found that there were many I disliked. I felt down about this at first until I accepted the fact that as much as I hated not being successful at something, I learned a lot of lessons. I am now working in a field that gives me energy, rather than draining me, is rewarding and is in line with all of my values. If it was not for my first attempt, I would have never had the courage to begin writing books and helping others discover and accomplish their dreams. I needed that experience and insight to be able to help others as I do today.

Understand the Theory of Sunk Cost

The term *sunk cost* is used both in the business field and in a psychological decision-making theory. It describes when people make decisions based on past costs (time, money, and effort) rather than future value. This mindset causes many people to stay in unhappy situations and prevents them from moving forward in new directions. For example, a person gets a law degree but finds that he hates practicing law. If he makes a decision based on sunk costs he will look for jobs practicing law because he spent years, effort and money studying law. Based solely on sunk costs he sees this as a better decision than pursuing a different field.

When pursuing your life purpose, it is imperative to not make decisions based on sunk costs. This will only hold you back and cause you to eventually end up in the same situation you are in now. Almost everyone has made at least one life decision using this process, and it may be uncomfortable to change your thinking at first. Keep this theory in mind anytime you find yourself sticking with something only because you spent time, money or effort on it. Ask yourself, are you making a decision because it will be the best for your future or are you doing it only because you feel you have wasted too much not to continue with it?

Remember This...

In completion of this chapter, I want to end with one final quote from Thomas Edison that states "Many of life's failures are people who did not realize how close they were to success when they gave up."

You never fail, as long as you learn and keep trying.

Part III: Methods to Guide this Process

This final section provides a list of techniques you can practice to assist you on your journey. Try them all or pick just one that resonates with you the most. The purpose of this section is to give you a wide range of tools to pick from. I have found in my own journey, the more tools you have, the easier it becomes. I have personally tried every technique listed below and found each to be immensely helpful in both changing my beliefs and moving towards my life purpose. I hope you find at least one here that is effective for you or at least encourages you to look elsewhere for additional techniques.

In this section you will find:

1. Manifesting and visualization methods
2. Meditation Techniques
3. List of Affirmations
4. Letter Technique

In addition, it will give you tips to find helpful support and of how to prevent others from disrupting your progress.

Chapter 18: Visualize and Manifest Your New Life

Manifesting has become a bit of a buzzword recently. Some believe in it, others are skeptical. In this chapter, I will explain the importance of using it as a visualization tool. There are plenty of additional resources that explain it in-depth if this is of interest to you. This chapter will explain how it can be used to change your subconscious thinking patterns as well as change the vibration of your energy.

Have you ever driven to work and had no idea how you got there? Kind of scary, right? Not really. Your subconscious has you covered. When you were first learning to drive a car, I am sure that you paid attention to every single move, making sure that you were doing everything correctly. Once you learned this, however, the mechanisms of how to drive a car are stored deep within your memory. This is why we can drive to work and think about our to-do list, a conversation we had two months ago, and what we are going to eat for lunch, instead of thinking about using our turn signals, remembering what different traffic signs mean, or making sure that we properly check our mirrors before changing lanes. This has all been ingrained, freeing our minds to focus on other things.

How great! Not always...

The problem with the ability of our complex brains to help us navigate the world so effortlessly is that often we can be lead down a path subconsciously that we do not want to travel. For example, have you ever reacted just like one of your parents, even when you consciously make an effort not to? This happens because these behaviors were ingrained in us from a young age. It may be easy to control them when we are fully conscious and mindful, yet when our minds arebusy, our subconscious takes over and acts in the ways that are congruent with its programming. The subconscious does not know any better. It does not weigh the pros and cons of decisions nor does it contemplate the right actions; these logical thinking techniques can only be done on a conscious level. We make far more decisions based on subconscious programming than we would like to think about.

That is scary! But there is hope...

Visualization and manifestation can help to change your subconscious programming so that you begin to live and act in ways that support the life you want. It takes work but it can be done. Much of your subconscious was formed before the age of two, and you have been reinforcing this programming ever since, with your decisions and through your cognitive biases, as mentioned previously. Knowing this, it may take a while to change it so patience is imperative. If you are consistent, you will begin to see more and more of the changes you desire. Visualization and manifestation are different than other techniques, such as affirmations or 'talking to your subconscious', because with these you will be using pictures instead of words to visualize the life you desire. If you desire success, you will visualize yourself as successful instead of simply saying "I am successful." The more vivid and concrete you get in your visualizations, the better. You may try to visualize all the components of living your life purpose such as the business you run, the car you drive, the house you live in, as well as all of the emotions that accompany your success. With time, you will begin to act in ways that make these dreams a reality. Let's look at an example of Susan to illustrate how to use visualization to change belief and behavior patterns which eventually leads to the desired outcome.

Current Situation of Lack: Susan grew up poor in a family of eight children. Her father was a coal miner and her mother a housewife. They lived in a rundown house, in a poor town, and she never owned a new piece of clothing her entire life. At an early age, Susan was programmed to believe she would never be rich. Fast-forward 30 years. Susan graduated college and law school, determined to get out of poverty. After lawschool, however, she had a lot of problems finding a decent paying job. On top of this, she had a lot of debt, from school and credit cards. She felt like she would never get ahead. No matter the choices that Susan made consciously, to further her education and better her situation, she still was driven to a life of lack. She could have made numerous decisions from a subconscious level that affected her current situation but is unable to recognize what they were. She decides to make a change.

Visualization: Susan begins visualizing herself getting an offer for a high paying job. She sees herself confidently applying for jobs and networking with the right people. She sees herself getting a call for an interview for her dream job and feels the overwhelming excitement. She then visualizes herself impressing the pants off her future boss who offers her the job on the spot. She next visualizes moving into her brand new office, incorporating the smells, the view, and her sense of accomplishment. And finally she visualizes receiving her large paycheck and feels the security and relief the money brings her.

Real Life Reward: After two months of visualizing, and not allowing herself to think any thoughts of lack or failure, she is invited to a networking event. Her 'old' self would likely have declined for various reasons, but she feels an urge to go. At this event, she meets the owner of one of the top law firms who is looking to replace an attorney who resigned that day. Susan talks to him, and they bond over attending the same undergraduate university. Even though she lacks experience, he tells her to come in for an interview. She feels a sense of courage and confidence she never felt before during that interview and two weeks later has the job.

How it Worked: Manifesting does not magically place money, abundance, love, or success into one's lap. It simply causes a person to make subtle decisions that have a ripple effect. Perhaps Susan was acting exceptionally confident and funny, making her coworker think it would be a good idea to take her as a guest to the networking event. In the past, she would have come up with a lot of excuses not to go, that to her seemed valid, but in reality were self-sabotaging. Because of her subconscious shift, she decided to go. Again, prior to the shift she may have never felt compelled to talk to this particular high-powered lawyer, let alone talk to him about her college days. This led to an opportunity that if presented two months prior, Susan would have been a nervous wreck and unable to showcase her skills and attributes. Because of her visualization, she was able to confidently interview and get the job offer.

An interesting characteristic about our subconscious is that it does not know the difference between real life and pretend. It only knows what it is being fed by your conscious experience. Your thoughts evoke feelings, and when a visual picture is paired with emotion, it reshapes your perception of reality. Susan once had a reality of lack and poverty but once her perception changed to perceive her life as successful and abundant the real world shifted to meet this perception. Life is all about perception. There are people who make $20,000 a year and see themselves as financially comfortable while others making six figures constantly see themselves as needing more. Alter your perception to always be that of abundance, love, and fulfillment and you will find your life purpose.

Manifesting can also be described using the Law of Manifestation, Law of Attraction or Law of Vibration. This explains the philosophyin which there is an energy that connects us with everything else in the universe and to manifest the reality you want,you need to first align your energy to that of which you desire. This is a theory based on quantum physics and metaphysics in which each thought is believed to be energy that attracts like energy to it. If you are emitting negative energy with your thoughts, you will attract the same type of negativity. If you emit loving energy with your thoughts, you will attract loving energy in return. This explanation defines the theory's premise, but there is plenty more information about the Law of Attractionavailable if you choose to research further. The process during energy manifesting is essentially the same as the manifesting visualization illustrated previously. As you shift your subconscious, you also shift your energy, affecting the decisions you make and what you essentially attract into your life.

Chapter 19: Six Powerful Meditation Techniques

I cannot speak enough to the power of meditation. Our worlds are constantly filled with stimulation, our minds are rarely without thoughts, and feelings of anger, stress, anxiety, and depression are present on a daily basis. Meditation gives you a break from all of this. It is helpful in discovering your life purpose in many ways. First, it slows your mind down making it easier to observe your thinking patterns. This helps you understand what thoughts are causing particular emotions (fear, doubt) that can prevent you from pursuing certain opportunities. It also helps with understanding what conditioned thinking patterns currently affect you.

Second, meditation helps you communicate with your subconscious. Pictureyourself in a crowded arena and you see a friend on the other side, you try to get his attention by shouting and waving your arms, yet because of all the noise and commotion your friend never sees you. Now, picture the arena is empty, and it is just you and him, he can easily see you and is able to hear everything you say. Your mind is the arena, and your subconscious is the friend on the other side. With all the constant chatter occurring in our minds, it can seem like a busy arena making it impossible to communicate with the subconscious. Meditation removes all the noise and makes this process much simpler.

Finally, meditation will clear your mind so you can effectively ponder what you actually should be doing. If you come home from a long day at work and have deadlines, finances, and an argument with a co-worker in your head, adding another task for your tired mind to process, pondering your life purpose, will be stress-inducing and seemingly impossible. You must clear out all of the junk before you can easily allow new thoughts to enter your mind.

There are multiple meditation techniques to use, and it is highly suggested you meditate before any of the activities listed in this book (journaling, researching, making lists, and brainstorming). Information on meditation can be found online, YouTube, or in books. You can also download mp3s or purchase CDs to get meditation music and directed or guided meditation. Below are brief descriptions of various techniques and how to use them specifically to find your life purpose.

Technique One: Mindful Meditation

Mindfulness meditation is the practice of clearing your mind and focusing on nothing but the here and now without judgment or trying to change anything. With the practice of daily meditation, it will be easier to control your stress and anxiety. You would not run a marathon without extensive training first, and mindfulness should be viewed similarly to any other training that helps you achieve the desired result. The more you work on it, the stronger your mindfulness power and endurance become. If you wish to develop a mindfulness meditation practice, it is best to start with shorter amounts of time and increase it. It is also best to pick the same time each day that you can commit to setting time aside to meditate. The more you can practice on a regular, consistent basis the better the overall results. Often people pick the morning to practice meditation or right before bed.

Use this type of meditation before any journaling, list making or making important decisions. Also use it to practice observing your thoughts without judging them.

Action Steps:

1. Find a comfortable place to either lie straight or sit up. (Sometimes sitting can be better as you will not likely fall asleep).

2. Set a timer. When you start out, it is best to keep it around 10 minutes, but you can certainly increase this as you feel fit.

3. Begin to take calm breaths. Pay attention to how your breathing feels going in your nose, down your lungs and back out of your nose. Pay attention to how your chest or stomach rises and falls as your breath. The crucial component is not to try to change your breathing or make any judgments. This is not a deep breathing exercise. Breathe normally and merely focus your attention on your breath and body.

4. Next, do a body scan. Start with the top of your head. How does it feel? What is the temperature? Can you feel your hair off your scalp? Now move down to your face. What do the back of your eyelids look like? How do your nose, lips, and chin feel? Continue this process down your entire body until you reach your toes. Pay attention to temperature and feeling. Notice if there is any tension or tightness but do not try to change or fix any sensation. You are simply noticing sensations and moving on.

5. After your body scan, pay attention to noises. First the sounds of your body. Can you hear your breathing? Focus just on that sound. Next, focus on the sounds in that room. What noises can you hear only in this space? Move on then to outside of that room, to the hallway or other areas of your living space. What noises can you hear? Finally, focus your attention past your living space to the outside. Can you hear anything?

6. Finally, pay attention to how it feels to be at that very moment. Let any thought that comes into your mind float out. Do not judge yourself for falling out of a mindfulness state and do not judge any thought that comes into your head. Do not attach any emotion to anything. Simply focus on sensations. A thought is solely a thought that floats in and out when no attention is paid to it.

7. If you find that one technique works best for you then carry out the rest of the meditation using that technique, if not just "be" until your timer rings.

Technique Two: Breathing Meditation

This is a great meditation for beginners. It helps to both focus and calm the mind, as well as physically relax the body. There are many different ways that you can engage in this type of meditation. It is best to set a timer so that you can focus exclusively on breathing without worrying about the time. It is a beneficial technique to engage in anytime you feel overwhelmed and is exceptionally easy because it can be done anywhere.

To prepare for the meditation, you can lie down or sit in a chair with your eyes open or closed. For a deeper relaxation, sitting or lying in a quiet space with your eyes closed is recommended. Take deep inhales into your diaphragm (your stomach) and exhale fully until all air is emptied from your body. Make sure that the breath is rhythmic and consistent each cycle (i.e. you breathe in and out for the same length of time each round). We are used to taking shallow breaths, into our chest, especially when we are under stress. Under stress our breathing can also be inconsistent, perhaps you take four shallow breaths, followed by one deep breath, followed by five shallow breaths, so on. During this meditation, inhale deeply until your belly rises and exhale fully as your stomach collapses and pulls in; the length of each breath is not nearly as important as the consistency throughout the meditation. Below is a brief list of different types of breathing you can engage in, but there are countless others that you can easily research:

1. Inhale/Hold/Exhale at Same Count: Inhale 4 count, hold 4count, exhale 4count, hold 4count, repeat

2. Exhale Longer than Inhale: Inhale 5 count, Hold 6 count, Exhale 7 count, Hold 6 count, repeat

3. Visualized Breathing: Picture a cleansing blue color clearing your mind and body as you inhale and picture a

red color as you exhale all of your built up stress, anxiety, doubt and any other negative feelings.

Technique Three: Progressive Muscle Relaxation

This is a meditation technique designed to fully relax your body. Your mind will also be focused on your body and not easily able to wander. There are 2 steps in this mediation, the first is to tense and contract your muscles and the second is to relax those same muscles. It is best to find a comfortable place and lie down in order to fully relax.

During this meditation, you will be working with all the major muscle groups in your body. To make it easy to remember, start with your feet and systematically move up or if you prefer, you can do it in the reverse order, from your forehead down to your feet. You can also choose to focus on each side of the body separately (for example tense left foot, relax, then tense the right foot, and relax) or together (tense both feet at the same time, then relax both at the same time). Use the below steps as a guide to first tighten each muscle, hold the contraction for a count of 1-5 seconds, and release fully:

1. Feet (curl your toes downward, point your toes), Hold, and Relax
2. Lower leg and foot (tighten your calf muscle by pulling toes towards you), Hold, and Relax
3. Entire leg (squeeze thigh muscles while doing above), Hold, and Relax
4. Hands (clench your fists), Hold, and Relax
5. Arms (tighten your biceps and forearms while clenching fist), Hold, and Relax
6. Buttocks (clench your buttocks together), Hold, and Relax

7. Stomach (pull your stomach in), Hold, and Relax

8. Chest (tighten entire chest), Hold, and Relax

9. Neck and shoulders (shrug your shoulders up to your ears), Hold, and Relax

10. Mouth (open your mouth wide), Hold, and Relax

11. Eyes (clench your eyelids tightly), Hold, and Relax

12. Forehead (raise your eyebrows), Hold, and Relax

13. Finish with Entire Body Tension, Hold, and Relax

Note: If you have any injuries, heart problems or other medical issues, consult your doctor before engaging in this activity.

Technique Four: Guided Meditation

Guided meditations are another great tool for beginners. During this, you listen to an audio guiding you deep into meditation. There are plenty available for free on YouTube or recordings available topurchase. You can also guide yourself through a meditation using your own thoughts, although it may be harder to relax and let go than if you were to listen to pre-recorded one. There are guided meditations specifically for commutating with your subconscious and for releasing old, negative thinking patterns. These are very similar to hypnosis, and some guided meditations will be labeled as hypnosis when searching online. The key to receiving the most benefit is to allow yourself to be open to deep relaxation and the suggestions stated in these guided meditations. The deeper you go in the meditation, the more positive effects you will experience.

Technique Five: Anchoring

Anchoring is aNeuro-Linguistic Programming, NLP, technique used to induce a frame of mind or emotion. It is a conditioning that develops when a person evokes an emotion and pairs it with a gesture or touch of some kind. To do this get into a meditative state. Use breathing, mindfulness or any combination to begin.

Then think of an emotion you want to condition. This could be success, happiness, fulfillment or relaxation. Now picture a time in your life when you experienced the desired emotion. If you aspire to feel successful, then think of a time in your life when you experienced success. Perhaps, it was when your football team won the state championships in high school, or you got the top grade in the class during college. Picture the moment vividly and experience the emotions as if they are currently happening. While feeling the emotion, hold your thumb and index finger together. Relax for a few seconds then reimagine this experience with a heightened state of emotion and again bring your thumb and index finger together. Repeat this process 3-5 additional times. If you repeat this exercise daily, eventually when you put your thumb and index finger together you will experience the emotion, no matter the circumstance.

You can use this technique as you are trying to re-condition your thinking. For example, if you anchor a feeling of success, anytime you are experiencing doubt or feelings of overwhelm, you can use your anchor to stimulate a positive, successful state. Anchoring can be used in conjunction with other visualization techniques as well. For example, once your anchor is set you can visualize yourself being asuccess in your current or future pursuits, engage the anchor by placing your thumb and finger together, and experience the emotional response to being successful making your visualization more real.

Technique Six: Imprinting New Beliefs

In this technique, you will get into a meditative state, with any of the exercises listed above and say a set of affirmations. Use the same set of statements every time and try to feel as if these affirmations are real. Somedays you may believe them and others your ego and lower-self may step in and call you a liar. It doesn't matter. The important part is that you are imprinting new beliefs into your subconscious. Do this for at least 5 minutes every day for a minimum of 30 days to start to see some results.

Chapter 20: Affirmations for Money, Success and Happiness

Affirmations, as previously discussed, are one of the main methods to change your conditioned beliefs and to restructure your subconscious. The power of affirmations lies in both repetition and accompanying appropriate feelings with the statements (i.e. if you state you are happy, feel happy as you say it).

Researchers and spiritual leaders have emphasized the impact that *"I am"* affirmations have in changing one's self-concept. Your self-concept is comprised of all the beliefs and 'truths' you hold about yourself. You will act in ways that support this concept, so when you want to change your life, you must change your self-concept by using these powerful *"I am"* statements. Use these specifically to change false or negative beliefs. Per the example listed in Part II, if you believe you are a failure, repeat the affirmation *"I am a success."* Also noted earlier, you may not believe the affirmation at first, but over time the statement will help to positively alter your self-concept.

As Louise Hay, one of the founders of the self-improvement movement, states:

"These affirmations are like fertilizing the soil of your mind, as you absorb them by repetition, you are slowly enriching the very basis of your garden of life. Anything you plant will grow abundantly."

You have planted seeds of negativity and doubt and grew a garden in your mind. It is time to tear out those unhealthy weeds, and replace them with new, healthy seeds using affirmations.

You can develop your own affirmations, find books of affirmations or lists online. There are also YouTube and mp3 audios you can download. Try to keep the statements brief and concrete and say them to yourself on a regular basis (at least once a day). The more you say them, the more effective they become, so think of times that you can add them into your day (upon awakening, when commuting, as you take a walk, or before bed). Below is a list of 50 Affirmations and "*I am*" statements to help you get started. You can use these to change your beliefs and assist in finding your life purpose.

Life Purpose:

I am living my life purpose.

I do what I love every day.

I am happy with my work.

I love living my life purpose.

I am filled with new ideas to live my life purpose.

I work joyfully towards my life purpose.

I am fulfilled and happy every day.

I am changing the world with my work.

I am progressing towards my life purpose every day.

I am doing amazing things with my life.

Success:

I am successful.

Everything I do turns into a success.

I work hard every day towards my success.

I am creative and successful.

Others see me as successful.

I live a life filled with success.

I see success in everything.

I am grateful for all of my success.

I love being successful.

I wake up feeling successful every morning.

Money:

I am wealthy.

I am abundant.

Money comes to me easily.

I love being rich.

I help others with my money.

I deserve to make a lot of money.

I enjoy all of the abundance life brings to me.

I make more and more money every day.

I spend money easily as I know I will always make more.

I invest money wisely.

Ability:

I accomplish anything I set my mind to.

I am smart.

I am determined.

I am capable of achieving my dreams.

I am unique and special.

I am always coming up with new ideas.

I am awesome.

I am persistent.

I never give up.

My hard work always pays off.

<u>Self-Love and Acceptance:</u>

I am amazing.

I am loved.

I am respected.

I am accomplished.

I am brave.

I am at peace.

I am balanced.

I am inspired.

I am deserving of all my dreams.

Others look up to me.

Chapter 21: Write a Letter to Yourself

A technique that holds you accountable as well as assists in manifesting and changing your thinking patterns is writing a letter to yourself that declares your goals and then reading it every day. Ideal times to read this letter are either in the morning or right before bed, as well as before any meditation. In this letter express where you want to be in a year, six months, three years, whatever feels right to you. You can add how much money you want to have earned, the position you will be in, the mindset you will have, and any personal goals. Write the letter as if you are your future self, talking to your present self. See the example for an illustration of what this might look like:

Dear Sam,

By January 1, 2018, I have a successful real estate business. I make over 150, 000 dollars a year. I have a balanced lifestyle in which I spend at least 2 hours with my wife and children every single day. I am planning to go on a 10-day vacation to Italy with my family. I wake up every morning excited about life and never let the little things affect me. I meditate for 20 minutes every day upon waking, exercise 3 times a week, and take mindful walks anytime I feel stress creeping up. I am happy, successful and abundant.

Sincerely,

Sam

Chapter 22: Find the Right Support

The journey to discover and pursues your life purpose can feel lonely at times. As you progress, your thinking patterns and views of yourself and the world will become increasingly different than that of the general public. You cannot expect others to change as you are changing, yet a support system can be crucial to your success. People who understand what you are trying to do will provide you with both encouragement and hold you accountable. You may begin this journey alone, but it will be hard to continue this sole effort as obstacles and challenges present themselves. Thus it is a good idea to find one or more individuals who can relate to your journey.

Finding a group of like-minded individuals who can provide encouragement, advice and accountability will help your life-purpose pursuits and your overall well-being. But how does one find such a support system?

Finding support can be less intimidating than it first appears. First, look to friends or family who you think may be receptive. Test the waters and strike up a broad conversation about what you have learned in this book. If they seem interested, then tell them a bit more, but if you sense judgment or skepticism, you will have to find support elsewhere. When searching for support outside of friends and family, try to find groups that have people who are at the same level as you, with similar interests and goals. Explore Meetups (www.meetup.com) in your city and/or online support groups. Begin to look at different online forums. You can start on platforms like Quora (www.quora.com) or Reddit (www.reddit.com) or search for specific platforms related to your goals. Here you are able to ask questions or simply read through other's questions and answers that relate to topics you are interested in. There are also tons of Facebook groups available to join. Do not be reluctant to join groups that are labeled "closed". Often if you request to join, they will accept your request. Also, don't feel pressured to participate immediately after joining a group. You can scope several out and explore the best fit before engaging. Through online groups, members will often form outside mastermind groups, kind of like study groups, where they talk periodically via skype, google hangout or on conference calls. You can keep an eye out for these opportunities or, as you become more comfortable, look into forming one yourself.

If you cannot find support, and life gets tough, do not allow yourself to deal with your battles alone. Look for a life coach, a counselor or free support groups located in your area to talk through hard times. There has been increased awareness of mental health and battling depression and anxiety in the entrepreneur community. Several famous entrepreneurs have even spoken out about dealing with depression and suicidal thoughts. When you are working towards success, some days are overwhelming. In these cases, you need someone to lean on. Being alone with your thoughts during a state of heightened stress or anxiety is detrimental to your success and possibly your future.

Chapter 23: Shhh! Keep Your Dreams a Secret at First

Have you ever told another person news that excited you and their reaction was less than enthusiastic? How did this make you feel? Likely irritated, angry, sad, or possibly caused you to question your own feelings of excitement. These negative thoughts and emotions will do nothing to help you achieve the success you desire so it can be best not to risk telling others at first. When you are in the phase of exploring your true desires, you may be tempted to scream it to the world because it is exciting but others may not understand your excitement. This process takes a lot of self-work, and it only takes one negative conversation to put you back in your progress.

Dr. Wayne Dyer, considered the "Father of Motivation", suggested to keep your desires a secret when you are trying to manifest them. In this book, *The Power of Intention,* he explains that when you set your intention, you have to know that your desires will come to fruition. You may not know when or how, but you must be certain they will. If you tell another person, they may have questions of "How?" and "When?" and "Why?' that can cause you to doubt yourself on a conscious or subconscious level. This will only inhibit the true manifestation of your desires.

Remember that others' doubts simply come from their own experiences andconditioning, and you cannot expect everybody to be on the same page as you. Always remember,with work you can achieve your life purpose no matter what others say. Once you are confident and certain you are on the path to living yourlife purpose, feel free to share your experiencewith everyone. Inspire others by your actions, not your words, and you may even motivate people close to you to embark on their own journey.

Chapter 24: Quick Recap

This book covered a lot of material. It was designed as a guide, but I know many prefer to read through new information completely before taking action. For this reason, I thought a brief recap would be beneficial. Let's review what you have learned:

1. Everyone develops dysfunctional thinking and behavior patterns due to experiences, learning and conditioning. Society, family and peers abide by a set of norms that often do not promote the discovery of living your life purpose.

2. The first step to make changes in your life is to understand how your conditioning and thinking patterns negatively affect you and prevent you from living your life purpose.

3. After you gain this understanding, you then must decide how you will change these dysfunctional patterns. (Affirmations, journaling, talking to your subconscious, meditation techniques)

4. Once you let go of the beliefs that hold you back, you can then begin to explore what career or business would align with your true self. This exploration process begins by examining your interests, strengths and values.

5. Once you have a list of ideas, develop a plan to research each one thoroughly. This is often the most important step.

6. Planning and goal setting will help you develop a strategy to both research and take action on your career or business ideas. Develop a plan for the next year and break it down into quarters. Set and accomplish daily SMART goals to help you stay on track.

7. Change your perception of failure and do not allow setbacks to stop you in this journey. Try and try again!

8. To assist in accomplishing goals, try manifesting or visualization techniques, writing a letter to yourself, in addition to meditation and saying daily affirmations.

9. Get support from the right people and do not allow others to discourage you.

10. Beware of: The Ego, Cognitive Distortions, Cognitive Biases, Unhealthy Subconscious Beliefs, Theory of Sunk Costs, "What if" and "But", Old Behavior and Thinking Patterns, and Naysayers. All of these will only sidetrack you from living the life you desire.

11. Remember this is a process and no two people will have the same journey. The key is to take back control of your thinking and your life.

Conclusion

"Watch your thoughts; they become words. Watch your words; they become actions. Watch your actions, they become habits. Watch your habits, they become character. Watch your character; it becomes your destiny." - Frank Outlaw

Welcome to the other side. You now have an understanding of what most do not. You questioned norms and decided to take the first steps into the unknown. I hope you are able to use the information presented in this book to discover and pursue your life purpose. I speak from personal experience in saying, it will be well worth it.

About the Author

I sat on the trolley every morning and evening commuting to and from work. To a job that required a Master's degree. A job that took six years in school with a 4.0 GPA and six months after graduating with my M.A. to get. A job that I moved and bought a house for and was very excited to begin. A job that quickly sucked the life out of me, yet I continued to work at for over four years. So, for over four years, I sat on that trolley and looked at the fellow commuters. They all looked miserable. I would sit there every day thinking *I do not want to be riding on this trolley for the remainder of my working years*. Nevertheless, I sat there year after year and never made a change. Often my co-worker and I would talk about the businesses we would want to open and how fun it would be to live a life other than one where we dreaded work each day. It always seemed like a nice dream to fantasize about but one that never seemed in reach. I remember telling my supervisor in grad school I just wanted a job I looked forward to working each day and she scoffed at the seemingly naïve comment. It seemed I always had this feeling there was more out there but I did not know what it was.

It was not until I moved to a new city that a shift began. I moved for a new, happy life but soon fell back into old routines, applying for jobs I was not passionate about for salaries far beneath what I wanted. A simple discussion with my boyfriend, in which he stated there should be more pet stores in our dog-friendly area, prompted my mind shift. I love animals. I had money from selling my house and I could be the one to open this pet store!

I began to explore opening a bricks and mortar pet boutique. The neighborhood I lived in was full of dogs and I was confident it would be a success. I went to the library and started to search for books about business. They all seemed so boring and dry, until I found one that drew me in. Through reading this book, I learned that people from all walks of life, with different passions, have been successful opening their own businesses. This gave me a boost of confidence.

I found a local non-profit that offered business classes for those interested in starting their own businesses (www.score.org). I went through a 6 week course and was excited about continuing on this journey. To get experience in management, I became a manager at a coffee shop and also a dog walker while I continued to plan and look for store locations. I found out quickly, that I did not like managing. I was always on call. I remember taking a weekend trip and getting 5 calls on the way up from employees. This made me begin to question what it would be like if I opened up my own place. It made me a little uneasy to think about not having the freedom to enjoy a weekend away when I wanted. While this was happening, I was also not having any luck finding a location for a store in my area. In talking with my business mentor, I decided it would be a good idea to look into starting an online store while I continued to look for locations. I began to research this a bit further and realized it would be feasible. I had to, however, make an entirely new business plan. I began this process planning for a physical location but online was a new beast.

My online pet boutique was up and running within a few months of me making this decision. It is not initially easy to drive traffic to an online business but I began to see the potential of having a business based online. There was freedom in this. I could work from anywhere and make my own schedule. Every single day, I read tons of information, watched YouTube videos instead of TV, and listened to business podcasts in the car, instead of the radio. I also began a personal journey that involved intense work on my anxieties and mindset. I learned about manifesting and subconscious reprogramming, and applied the techniques. I became very honest with myself about what I truly wanted, and what personal traits and thoughts were holding me back from this. In the course of a year, I completely transformed.

I loved to tell my friends and family all the things I was learning and applying. I had some hiccups with my online pet boutique, due to manufacturer issues, and during this time re-evaluated what I truly wanted to do. Selling adorable animal products is fun but I wanted something more. Many online entrepreneurs have several businesses and I began to ponder what I could do next. I kept hearing about people fulfilling their "life purpose" and contemplated what that would look like for me. With my background in Psychology and Counseling, I felt compelled to help others. What a waste it would be for me to spend hours every day learning and developing all of these business and self-improvement techniques and not share them with anyone. Then I received a sign.

I was doing dishes, binge watching YouTube videos, when a video came on about writing and publishing books. I have always loved to write. I sat down and watched the video and I was filled with excitement. I then searched for more free information online. I found Facebook groups where I learned from others doing this. I purchased several courses before beginning on this adventure. Everything about it just felt *right*. I can help others, use my formal background and education in Psychology, all my experience in starting and running a business, and do something I felt passionate about.

I understand that becoming an entrepreneur is about overcoming internal barriers as much as it is overcoming external barriers. My goal is to teach others how to overcome both. I share this long journey of mine to let you know it is not always a simple and straight road to success, but with the right tools and mindset you can get there. I hope to provide much more information with you on your road to success.

If you decided you want to start a business but need some help, check out: **How to Start a Business: Everything You Need to Know to Start a Successful Business Today**

3 Books in 1: Including Seeds of an Entrepreneur, Startup Essentials and Just Right (Discover the Best Business for You). Here's what you will learn:

- Mindset and habits needed to become a successful entrepreneur
- Step-by-step guide to start a successful business
- Everything you need to know to find your perfect business idea

Available on Kindle!

Seeds of an Entrepreneur: Simple Guide to Change your Habits, Start your Business and Live a Life of Success

The primary focus of this book is to help you make the necessary mindset and lifestyle changes needed to take the leap into entrepreneurship. It is not a Business 101 book, but will help you build your confidence and develop habits to increase your chance of success and happiness as you prepare to start a business.

Is This Book Right for Me?

If you want more out of life but are unsure of the next steps, you are tired of working a 9-5 job with little room for advancement, want more freedom, want more money, want to discover what you are passionate about or if you want to learn how to turn your passions into a successful business this book will help you.

Startup Essentials

About the Book

It can be stressful to think about starting a business. There is so much that goes into it and finding a place to start can be very overwhelming. This simple guide goes through all the components you will need to know to start any business (online, retail, small business, home-based). It was written by someone who was in your exact same position, only a couple of years ago. It breaks down difficult concepts into simple, actionable steps that you can apply today. It also provides credible links to free resources for additional information, webinars, and templates needed to start a business (not affiliated with author or book).

Just Right: Discover the Best Business Idea for YOU!

Have you ever dreamed of getting out of the day-to-day grind and starting your own business? A recent survey found that 40 percent of people who wanted to become entrepreneurs did not pursue their dreams because they didn't have any ideas. And almost 50 percent stated they were reluctant because of finances. If you fall into one of these categories or if you are simply curious about what type of business will be right for you, this book provides those answers.

You will find 10 business categories, specific examples listed in each category, followed by a list of pros and cons for each type of business. Far too many entrepreneurs start businesses blindly and struggle or fail as a result. Even more people never start a business because of fear. You will discover that it is possible for you to turn your skills, passions and talents into a business as well as the type of business that will be your ideal fit.

Worried about money?
Find businesses you can start for free!

No idea where to start?
Get information to guide your next steps.

Afraid of failure?
Learn which businesses have the highest chance of success.
And how to prevent failure in any type of business.

The average person is simply unaware of all the opportunities in the business world. It is a well-kept secret that keeps many feeling stuck in unfulfilling jobs without seeing a way out. Use this book to open your eyes and take your first step to a better life today!

Here's a sneak peak at a few of the options we will cover:

- Online Business
- Retail Business
- Franchises
- Creative Business
- Service Business
- Passive Income
- Home-Based Business
- Nonprofits
- And many more!

References

Dyer, Dr. Wayne. *The Power of Intention.* Hay House (2005). Print.

Forleo, M. (2012).How to Reprogram Your Subconscious Mind to Get What You Want.*Marie Forleo.com.* Retrieved August 10 fromhttp://www.marieforleo.com/2012/09/your-subconscious-mind/

Grohol, J. (2016). What is Catastrophizing?. Psych Central. Retrieved on August 15, 2016, from http://psychcentral.com/lib/what-is-catastrophizing/

Grohol, J. (2016). 15 Common Cognitive Distortions. Psych Central. Retrieved on August 18, 2016, from http://psychcentral.com/lib/15-common-cognitive-distortions/

Hammond, J.S., Keeney, R. L., Raiffa, H. (1998). The Hidden Traps in Decision Making.*Harvard Business Review.* Retrieved August 22, 2016, www.hbr.com.

Josa, C. (2012). How to Use Anchoring to Help with Your Meditation.*Clara Josa.* Retreived August 20, 2016 fromhttp://www.clarejosa.com/articles/inspirational-messages/how-to-use-anchoring-to-help-with-your-meditation/

McGregor, J. (September 2, 2014). The Average Work Week is Not 47 Hours. *The Washington Post.*Retrieved on August 1, 2016 from https://www.washingtonpost.com/news/on-leadership/wp/2014/09/02/the-average-work-week-is-now-47-hours/

Miller, P. (April 27, 2014). Louise Hay-Affirmations and Power Thoughts. Retrieved from https://www.youtube.com/watch?v=tsgoG2UrxVM

www.ingramcontent.com/pod-product-compliance
Lightning Source LLC
Chambersburg PA
CBHW071822200526
45169CB00018B/703